# A River Journey

Acknowledgments
Executive Editor: Diane Sharpe
Supervising Editor: Stephanie Muller
Design Manager: Sharon Golden
Page Design: Simon Balley Design Associates
Photography: Bruce Coleman: cover (left and middle right),
pages 11, 12, 15; Robert Harding Picture Library: cover (top right),
pages 23, 26–27; Image Bank: pages 17, 25; Oxford Scientific
Films: pages 18–19, 21; Tony Stone: page 28; Zefa: page 7.

ISBN 0-8114-3789-2

Copyright © 1995 Steck-Vaughn Company.

1 2 3 4 5 6 7 8 9 00 PO 00 99 98 97 96 95 94

# A
# River
# Journey

Paul Humphrey and Alex Ramsay

*Illustrated by*

Lynda Stevens

®
STECK-VAUGHN
C O M P A N Y
ELEMENTARY • SECONDARY • ADULT • LIBRARY

It started as a stream high up in the hills.
Up there the stream flows very fast.

Like most rivers, our river flows
into the ocean.

That waterfall is only about 30 feet high. The world's highest waterfall is in Venezuela in South America. It is more than 3,000 feet high!

Let's go farther downstream to the boat. Then we can journey down the whole river.

The water in rivers and streams always flows down a valley.

Now the water is flowing much more slowly than it was higher up in the hills.

Many streams have joined ours.

Our stream is nearly big enough to be a river now.

Yes, we'll be sleeping in it for the next three or four days.

No, ducks' feathers are covered with
oil to keep water out. The ducks are
quite dry and warm underneath.

What is that animal on the riverbank?

That's an otter. We're lucky to see it.
Otters are quite rare.

12

It lives in a hole in the bank. Otters have webbed feet like frogs. They are very good swimmers.

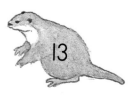

13

Yes, the river is nice and clean here, so there are many fish to catch.

That's a heron. It's the best fisher of all.
It uses its long, sharp beak to catch food.

That's an old mill. Years ago that was where wheat was ground into flour for making bread.

 16

The river turned the wheel, which turned
the grinding machinery inside the mill.

17

That's from the town we just passed
through. Why don't we collect some
with our nets?

No, they don't. They can be hurt by trash left in the water. When the water is dirty, very few river animals can live in it.

Look, everybody. We're coming to
a dam.

Do you see those big gates? They are lock gates. Our boat will go into the lock and be gently lowered as the water is let out. Then we will go out the other end.

It's like a staircase in the river.

That's right. Boats can go up a lock as
well as go down.

Do you see how wide the valley is now?

It's called a suspension bridge. It hangs from strong steel wires fastened to those tall towers.

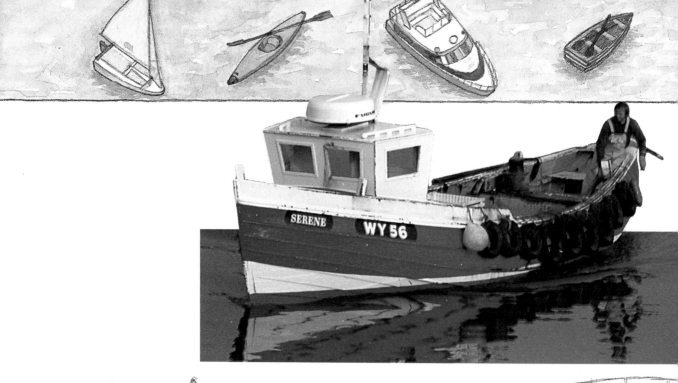

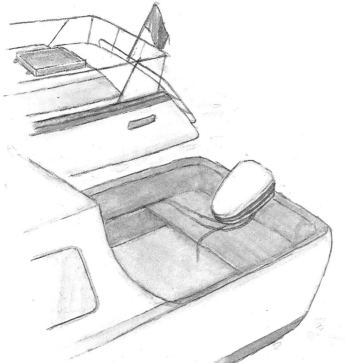

We're going through a big town now.

This is a busy port. Can you see the
fishing boats?

These ships are too big to sail up the river, aren't they?

Yes, they unload their cargoes at the dock. Then the cargoes are carried inland by trucks and trains.

Now our river journey is over. How many things can you remember? The answers are on the last page, but don't look until you have tried naming everything.

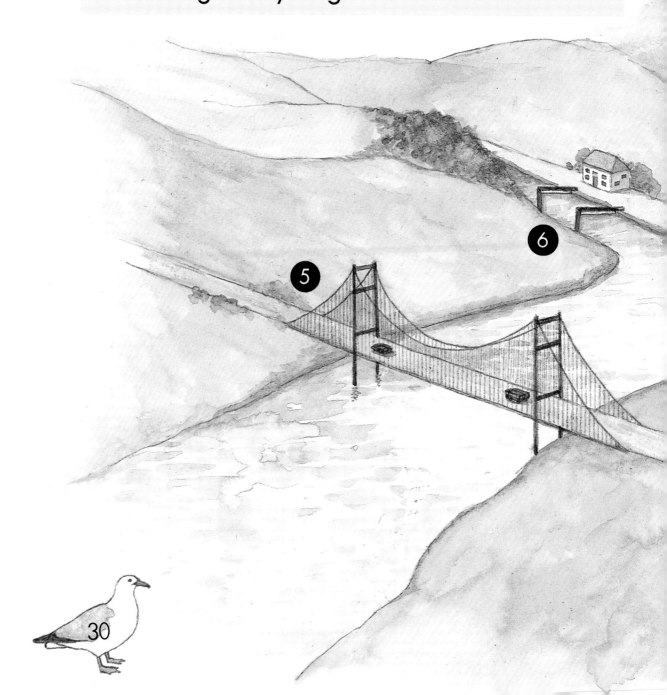

## Index

Answers: 1. Waterfall  2. Dam  3. Mill  4. Heron  5. Suspension bridge  6. Lock

32